Charles Seely of Lincoln

Liberalism and Making Money in Victorian England

Mark Acton and Stephen Roberts

Published under the imprint *Lincolnshire Lives*

Printed by Kindle Direct Publishing

© Mark Acton and Stephen Roberts, 2019

All rights reserved. No part of this publication may be reproduced in any form, stored in or re-introduced into a retrieval system, or transmitted, in any form or by any means, electronic, mechanical, photocopying, recording or otherwise without the prior consent of the authors.

The moral right of Mark Acton and Stephen Roberts to be identified as the authors of this work has been asserted in accordance with the Copyright, Designs and Patents Act 1988.

ISBN: 978-1796273823

Front cover: The Brayford wharfs, Lincoln.

For Andrew Walker

Contents

Contents i

Acknowledgements ii

I. 'The Baker's Boy' 1

II. 'A Liberal of the First Water' 9

III. An Entrepreneur 17

IV. 'The Naval Reformer' 26

V. At Home 35

VI. Last Years 42

Illustrations 47

Index 57

About the Authors 59

Acknowledgements

We have benefitted from the help of a number of people whilst working on this book. Thanks are due to Rob Wheeler for reading the third chapter and making a number of helpful suggestions for improvement. For answering queries and providing information we are grateful to: Daphne Denaro Brooke-Smith; Sue Curtis; Sarah Dawson; Dennis Mills; Kathryn Rix; Jon Sass; Sarah Seely; and Neil Wright and members of the Society for Lincolnshire History and Archaeology's industrial archaeology team. Any shortcomings and errors in this book are our responsibility.

We would like to record our gratitude to the staff of Lincolnshire Archives. We have also made extensive use of the British Newspaper Archive. For his time and technical expertise an acknowledgement is owed to Richard Brown. Our thanks also to the National Portrait Gallery and Brook Village History on the Isle of Wight for permission to reproduce a number of images. All other images reproduced in this book are from the authors' collections.

I. 'The Baker's Boy'

Charles Seely died at his country house on the Isle of Wight on 21 October 1887, leaving a personal estate valued at £496,901 4s 8d and a real estate reckoned to be worth £2,000,000.[1] He owned more land on the Isle of Wight than anyone else. He had been a Member of Parliament for a quarter of a century, a Justice of the Peace in three counties and a Deputy Lieutenant for two. His son, also Charles Seely, became a baronet. One grandson won the Distinguished Service Order in the Boer War, became Secretary of State for War and entered the peerage. A great-grandson served as a junior minister in Winston Churchill's wartime government and was also granted a barony. At the time of writing Charles Seely's great-great-great-grandson is the MP for the Isle of Wight. Whilst it would be an exaggeration to describe Charles Seely's story as one of rags to riches, it was nonetheless a remarkable rise for a man born the son of a provincial tradesman.

Charles Seely was born on 3 October 1803, the son of Charles who ran a bakery and flour dealing business at 261 High Street, Lincoln. The premises had been used by a succession of bakers since around 1672. A Seely baking dynasty had been founded by John who died in 1710. His widow Ellen bought the range of buildings of 16-18 Strait, Lincoln, which she left to her son William (died 1750) on her death in 1735.[2] In 1783 the widow of a later William put the property up for auction, though it was not until January 1787 that a John Stephenson announced that he had taken over the 'bake house and shop of the late Mr Seely'.[3] It seems unlikely therefore that Charles Seely senior was a son of William and his exact origins remain open to conjecture. He had certainly been the occupier of 261 High Street since 1798, perhaps as early as 1793.[4] He had married Ann, daughter of John Wilkinson, a Lincoln grocer and, as well as Charles, had a daughter, also Ann, who in 1826 married John Norton, a Lincoln draper. Charles Seely

---

[1] *Isle of Wight County Press*, 26 November 1887. *Hampshire Independent*, 22 October 1887.
[2] C. Johnson & S. Jones, *Steep, Strait and High* (Woodbridge, 2016), pp. 114-5.
[3] *Stamford Mercury*, 5 January 1787.
[4] C. Johnson & S. Jones, *Steep, Strait and High* (Woodbridge, 2016), p. 156.

senior died aged 41 after a long illness in 1809. His widow not only continued the business but in February 1815 bought the Hob Hole post windmill on Lincoln's Burton Road for £430 after the bankruptcy of its previous owner Thomas Bell.[5] She ran the mill in her own name until transferring ownership to her son on 10 August 1843. In March 1824 Ann Seely paid £420 for a piece of pasture land on Salthouse Lane in the parish of St Peter-at-Gowts in Lincoln. Sometime after 1828 she built a five-sailed windmill of nine storeys which she then sold to Dennis Lilly of Newark and Thomas Hibbert of Lincoln, both millers and bakers, for £1400 in 1841. This mill, now known as Le Tall's, survives though converted to residential use.[6]

There is little that can be said about Charles Seely's childhood. An obituary stated that he had attended Lincoln Grammar School, then sited in the Greyfriars building, where the boys learned Latin and Greek along with writing and arithmetic (accounts) together with some geography, geometry and astronomy.[7] He is also said to have convalesced with an aunt on the Isle of Wight when he determined, whilst walking on the downs above Mottistone, that once his fortune was made he would buy all the land between the downs and the sea.[8]

Seely's first business partner was John Coupland. Born around 1789, Coupland was listed in a trade directory of 1826 as a merchant and maltster.[9] From 1838 he served a three year term as an alderman on Lincoln town council.[10] For some years he farmed at Skellingthorpe, east of Lincoln, giving up in 1845 after paying £60,000 at auction for an estate of 2,200 acres at Broughton in north Lincolnshire, though he continued to live in Skellingthorpe Hall until his death.[11] In 1826 Coupland and Seely were announcing the erection of a steam engine 'for the purpose of

---

[5] *Stamford Mercury*, 25 November 1814 & information from Jon Sass.
[6] Ruth Tinley, 'Crown Mill, Lincoln', *Lincolnshire Past & Present*, vol. 36 (1999), pp. 7-10.
[7] Isle of Wight County Press, 29 October 1887. C. Garton, *Schola Lincolniensis: Lincoln School: A Summary Honours Board* (Lincoln, 1988).
[8] D. Brooke-Smith & S. Mears, *Brook: A Village History* (Newport, 2010), p. 89.
[9] *Lincolnshire Chronicle*, 9 February 1855. *White's History & Directory of Lincolnshire & Hull* (1826).
[10] Lincolnshire Archive Office Misc. Dep. 531/1.
[11] *Lincolnshire Chronicle*, 5 September 1845, 3 October 1845.

crushing bones and rape cake, for manure' and that they had on hand 'a quantity of bones of all sorts, ready ground'.[12] Their names were also linked as subscribers to the Association for the Protection of Property in the City, Bail and Close of Lincoln.[13] In October 1826 Coupland and Seely were advertising for 'two very good millers; likewise an engineer, to work a steam-engine'.[14]

On 28 June 1831 Charles Seely married, in St Andrews' Church, Newcastle upon Tyne, Mary Hilton, fourth daughter of the late Jonathan Hilton, a grocer of that city.[15] They were to have six children, but only four survived into adulthood. In the same year, in an early sign of civic activity, Seely was listed amongst the attendees at a meeting in Lincoln's Guildhall which resolved to promote a school for the infant poor.[16] In July 1833 his name appeared amongst subscribers towards a fund to help a Mrs Shuttleworth, a widow with eleven children, whose farm had been destroyed by fire. Seely gave ten shillings, as did John Coupland.[17] Mary Seely was also involved in charitable activity. She was listed amongst subscribers and benefactors to the Lincoln Dorcas Charity which sold clothing at half-price to the poor.[18] In December 1833 Seely attended the first public meeting of the members of the Lincoln and Lincolnshire Mechanics' Institution. He supported an unsuccessful attempt to allow rules to be changed by a simple majority rather than by two-thirds of members as originally proposed. Seely was elected to the Committee along with his friend Thomas Cooper, who was to become a well-known Chartist, though they seem only to have served for one year.[19]

Seely took on his first civic post in August 1834 when he became a commissioner for the parish of St Peter-at-Gowts under the Lincoln Lighting and Paving Act, holding office for three years. John Coupland also became a commissioner, though for the parish

---

[12] *Stamford Mercury*, 28 April 1826, 5 May 1826.
[13] *Stamford Mercury*, 24 March 1826.
[14] Ibid., 6 October 1826.
[15] *Newcastle Chronicle*, 2 July 1831. *Newcastle Courant*, 5 September 1807.
[16] *Stamford Mercury*, 24 June 1831.
[17] Ibid., 12 July 1833.
[18] Ibid., 13 December 1833.
[19] Ibid., 3 January 1834. 11 December 1835. Also see S. Roberts, *The Chartist Prisoners: The Radical Lives of Thomas Cooper (1805-92) and Arthur O'Neill (1819-96)* (Oxford, 2008), p.46.

of St Botolph's.[20] The first press mention of Thomas Michael Keyworth as a business partner of Seely's, is in 1836. Keyworth's father, John, had been managing clerk in the Smith Ellison bank. On retirement he had gone into business with his sons.[21] By 1828 they were maltsters and merchants in coal, linseed and rape cake.[22] They also had a wine and spirit business into which Seely must have become a partner as Keyworth and Seely announced that they had disposed of their stock to John Spendlow whilst requesting their friends to continue to trade with them in coal and malt at their Brayford premises.[23] Spendlow did not remain in business for long. In December 1836 Keyworth and Seely announced that they had re-taken their wine vaults before selling them to Richard Whitton junior. They continued to run their spirit vaults though they were trying to sell the business and its premises the following year. [24]

On 20 January 1837 a meeting took place in Lincoln's Guildhall to discuss the raising of a petition in favour of the abolition of church rates. Though he did not speak, Charles Seely was elected to the committee to pursue the matter along with John Coupland and Thomas Keyworth.[25] In May 1837 a press report said that Seely, 'a spirited young merchant', had begun a club 'in which some of the principal mercantile names of Lincoln [were] enrolled'. At its first meeting 'ten persons of known reform principles' gave in their names for £100 each 'towards prosecuting any case of bribery on the part of the Tories in the event of an election'.[26] In July 1837 Walter Cape was found guilty of the theft of some metal from the steam mill Keyworth and Seely had recently erected on the edge of Brayford Pool. He was given two month's imprisonment and hard labour.[27] A serious accident occurred in the steam mill in November 1837. Thomas Gould, married with nine children, was cleaning the wheels and shafts of the mill when the cuff of his greatcoat became entangled with the gear and his arm

---

[20] Ibid., 15 August 1834.
[21] F. Hill, *Georgian Lincoln* (Cambridge, 1966), pp 203-4.
[22] *Pigot & Co. Directory* (1828-9).
[23] *Stamford Mercury*, 18 March 1836.
[24] Ibid., 23 December 1836. 20 January 1837.
[25] Ibid., 27 January 1837.
[26] Ibid., 26 May 1837.
[27] *Lincolnshire Chronicle*, 28 July 1837.

was crushed. It was amputated above the elbow the same day.[28] The same month a boat laden with corn belonging to Keyworth and Seely was sunk in an accident at Bardney lock, downstream from Lincoln.[29]

1838 saw Seely paying £3,675 for granaries in South Square, Boston, which were formerly the property of Samuel Sandars, a corn merchant. It was suggested that Seely would build a steam mill there to carrying on a grinding business, though there is no evidence that he ever did so. In 1847 Seely paid a further £500 for a piece of land to the north of his Boston site which became a coal yard. Whilst Seely kept an office in Boston Market Place for his commercial activity, he let out the South Square property to various corn and timber merchants before selling out to Lestor Daulton, a Boston merchant, for £3,000 in 1865. [30]

On the evening of Monday, 15 April 1839 Charles Seely was walking along the banks of the River Witham in the Boultham area of Lincoln when he sprained his ankle. Whilst sitting down to recover he was approached by Richard Ellison, owner of the Boultham estate, who challenged him with the words 'what are you doing there like a scoundrel?' Seely stood up and asked why he had been spoken to in such a manner upon which Ellison knocked off Seely's hat with his sword and made a thrust with a dagger at his chest which Seely parried with his arm, causing the blade to go in up to the hilt and sever the interosseous artery. Seely then identified himself and asked Ellison for help. The latter bandaged the wound with his handkerchief and Seely was taken home to be treated by the surgeons Hewson and Brooke. An apology was tendered by Ellison on the Wednesday. He excused himself for being armed on the grounds that robbers were feared in the area, a man having recently been assaulted and robbed on the bridge at Boultham. [31]

A week later, Seely was described as still in a 'precarious state'. The Liberal *Stamford Mercury* claimed that no robbery had occurred in Boultham. The Tory *Lincolnshire Chronicle* continued to claim that 'attacks of so murderous a nature [in] the last few

---

[28] Ibid., 17 November 1837.
[29] Ibid., 1 December 1837.
[30] *Stamford Mercury*, 7 September 1838, 30 November 1838 & information from Neil Wright.
[31] *Stamford Mercury*, 19 April 1839 & *Lincolnshire Chronicle*, 19 April 1839.

years' made Ellison's carrying of arms justifiable. Both papers professed concern that partisans of the Liberal Seely and the Tory Ellison were using the incident to further their own ends.[32]

In June 1839 it was reported that Seely had begun legal action against Ellison, retaining the MP for Newark Thomas Wilde as his counsel. The case was to be heard at a court in Middlesex allowing the trial to be heard in front of a 'metropolitan jury'.[33] The following month it was rumoured that Ellison had made 'some overtures of settlement' to which Seely had replied that if Ellison resigned from the magistracy, opened the road from Gowts bridge as a public footpath and paid his medical bills then he would stop legal proceedings. The *Stamford Mercury*, though calling Seely's terms 'rather stiff', thought that they showed 'no selfish feeling and that if they were accepted the public would be the only gainers. [34] A week later the *Lincolnshire Chronicle* claimed that the report and the 'tyrant-audacity and monstrousness of the propositions' were such as to lead it to the conclusion that the *Mercury*'s piece was a 'gross and malicious calumny'.[35]

With no settlement reached between Seely and Ellison the case appeared at the Court of Common Pleas before its Chief Justice Sir Nicholas Tindal. Whilst Seely wished to have the hearing held in Middlesex, Ellison had succeeded in having it changed to Lincoln. Serjeant Wilde, for Seely, argued that a hearing in Lincoln would be unfair as Seely's opposition to the Corn Laws had caused 'strong prejudice' from the local farmers and that 'statements had been made that [Seely] was desirous of murdering farmers, by starving them, and that he had therefore received no more than his due'.[36] The court declined Seely's application for a hearing in Middlesex, speaking in 'unmeasured terms of the honesty and impartiality of Lincolnshire juries'. The case was set to be heard at Lincoln's March 1840 assizes.[37]

Seely's action to recover damages was held before a special jury and presided over by the Lord Chief Justice Lord Denman.

---

[32] *Stamford Mercury*, 26 April 1839 & *Lincolnshire Chronicle*, 26 April 1839.
[33] *Stamford Mercury*, 14 June 1839.
[34] Ibid., 5 July 1839.
[35] *Lincolnshire Chronicle*, 12 July 1839.
[36] *Stamford Mercury*, 22 November 1839.
[37] Ibid., 28 February 1840.

Seely's counsel, Frederic Hill, stated that his client was still suffering from some paralysis nearly a year on and that he could write only with great difficulty. Hill believed that Ellison had had no malicious intention towards Seely or intentionally wounded him but believed himself to be in danger though it was a pity that Ellison had carried a weapon. After Lord Denman had ventured that, with no malice attributed or 'imputation upon the character of either party', it might have been for a settlement to have been reached without recourse to the verdict of a jury, evidence was given by John Hewson, the surgeon who had treated Seely. For Ellison, Serjeant Goulburn said that the 'accidental injury' sustained by Seely was the 'result of a mischance' caused by the 'hasty and extraordinary conduct of the plaintiff himself'. He hoped that the jury would be of the opinion that Ellison had 'drawn his dagger against a supposed robber'.

Denman, in summing up, referred to two letters written by Ellison to Seely in the days after the incident: the first 'distinguished by gentlemanly and appropriate feelings'; the second, thought Denman, ought to have provided an explanation of his conduct which might have seen compensation without recourse to trial. He considered that Seely's injuries were more likely to have been received by a blow from Ellison rather than by Seely pushing against the blade. Denman told the jury that if they were of the opinion that Ellison had committed the assault and not established the justification of self-defence then Seely would be entitled to their verdict. This they agreed after an hour's consideration and awarded damages of £300 to Seely.[38]

It is not clear whether Charles Seely and Richard Ellison knew each other at the time of the assault. Though both were prominent citizens of Lincoln, Seely being then a town councillor whilst Ellison was a magistrate, a militia officer and a landed proprietor, they were unlikely to have associated socially or politically. Seely was an advanced Liberal with lower middle class origins. Ellison, the illegitimate son of a former MP for Lincoln, had been provided with the Boultham estate upon his marriage in 1830. The Ellisons had made their money from banking and the lease of the Fossdyke navigation. They had twice married into the Sibthorp family of Canwick and were to be counted as Tories.

---

[38] Ibid., 13 March 1840.

At the trial Frederic Hill had expressed 'surprise that the action had been the subject of much party observation and party feeling' and had been told that it was likely to be judged 'not by the facts ... but as parties agreed with the political opinions of the one side or another'.[39] It is reasonable to suppose that without the political differences between the two men and their supporters and the animosity between the *Lincolnshire Chronicle* and the *Stamford Mercury*, a compensation settlement would have been reached without legal action.

---

[39] Ibid., 13 March 1840.

II. 'A Liberal of the First Water'

Charles Seely was first elected to Lincoln's town council in November 1837. This body had been created by the Municipal Corporations Act of 1835 and replaced the old corporation which had been recruited by co-option from the city's freemen. It had few responsibilities beyond its properties and charities and its impact on Lincoln's citizens was mostly ceremonial. It did not set rates. These were still collected by parishes.

The new council consisted of eighteen councillors representing two wards who were elected by rate-paying householders. Councillors were elected for three-year terms with one-third of the council to be elected annually. The councillors could then elect six aldermen either from their own ranks or from qualified electors. The first elections in Lincoln saw a clean sweep by Whigs and radicals with only four members of the old council returned.[1]

Seely's election to the town council was to be far from straightforward. He was elected in place of William Rudgard who had been created an alderman following the death of Robert Fowler, the first mayor of the reformed council. At the time the town clerk advised that the ensuing vacancy for a councillor need not be filled in the short time. The seat was therefore left vacant until the scheduled elections in November.[2] Seely received 266 votes to serve for one year for the Minster ward.[3] A Tory, Frederick Kent, had also been elected for the Minster ward but the radical assessors in charge of the election had disallowed his return on the grounds that, as the surgeon for the police and city gaol, he was a paid employee of the council. They had declared William Dawber elected in his place.[4] At the council meeting on 10 November the Tory councillor Robert Swan announced that the returns of Dawber and Seely would be challenged by law, the latter allegedly because Seely had been sworn in before the proper time. The Tories applied for a writ of *quo warranto* which obliged Seely to prove that

---

[1] See F. Hill, *Victorian Lincoln*, pp. 38-43, for the early history of the new council.
[2] *Stamford Mercury*, 24 February 1837.
[3] *Stamford Mercury*, 3 November 1837.
[4] F. Hill, *Victorian Lincoln* p. 43.

his election had been lawful.[5] These were of course early days for elected councils and neither the councillors nor the town clerks whose duty it was to advise them were sure of the exact details of the 1835 Act. The Liberal *Stamford Mercury*, whose Lincoln correspondent was Seely's friend Thomas Cooper, had no doubt that the objections to Seely were entirely party political.

On 18 November, at the Bail Court in London, Sir Frederick Pollock, former and future Attorney-General, asked 'for a rule calling upon [Seely] to show cause why a writ of *quo warranto* should not issue, commanding him to show by what authority he held the office of one of the town council of the city of Lincoln.' It was contended that the vacancy in February should have been filled within fourteen days. The presiding judge upheld Pollock's application.[6]

In what may well been an attempt to limit legal costs Seely tried to resign his council seat. A letter from him to that effect was read out at the council meeting on 29 November but after discussion it was decided that this was not legally possible and that the decision must be decided by law.[7] It was not until 25 October 1838 that the council was informed that the Court of Queen's Bench had declared Seely's election illegal. Seely told the mayor and councillors that the whole proceedings had cost him £39 and that he hoped the council would reimburse him.[8] A few days later he was legally returned to the council, topping the poll for the Minster ward to serve a three-year term.[9]

In addition to attending quarterly meetings of the town council Seely served two years on the finance committee and one year on the watch committee. For three years he was a commissioner of sewers and a trustee of highways responsible for repairs. In July 1839 he joined a committee to negotiate with Richard Ellison of Sudbrooke (cousin of Richard Ellison of Boultham) over his interest in the Fossdyke Navigation. In January 1841, whilst mayor, Seely became a governor of Christ's Hospital School, of the Free Grammar School and of the county hospital.[10]

---

[5] *Stamford Mercury*, 10 November, 17 November 1837.
[6] *Morning Post*, 20 November 1837.
[7] *Stamford Mercury*, 1 December 1837.
[8] *Lincolnshire Chronicle*, 2 November 1838.
[9] *Stamford Mercury*, 2 November 1838.
[10] Lincolnshire Archive Office Misc. Dep. 531/1.

Seely identified himself as a Liberal. An issue which greatly concerned Liberals was unnecessary expenditure. Some of Seely's local concerns can be gleaned from the 'Lincoln Municipality' reports in the *Stamford Mercury*. In 1839 he contended that the council's annual grant of £50 to Lincoln races was illegal and not money spent for a necessary purpose. He gave notice that he would propose the pulling-down of the race-stand and the selling of its materials and considered that the races 'further[ed] immorality and irreligion' and added to the 'calendar of criminals'.[11] In the same year Seely persuaded the council that its subscriptions to public charities and institutions should be voted on annually as, with its membership changing, it should not tie down future councillors to such payments. He also raised what he considered to be the inefficient management of the upper department of the Grammar School which was under the control of the Dean and Chapter of Lincoln Cathedral. Evidently the Dean and Chapter were still paying the masters of the school the rates set at the school's incorporation in 1583 and leaving the Council to make up for the subsequent change in the value of money. Seely also alleged that 'many stones-weight' of books from the school's old classical library had been sold as waste paper.[12] In 1840 Seely's concern for council expenditure resurfaced when he called attention to the cost of gas used by an illuminated clock and various lights and lamps at the Stonebow and Guildhall. Measures were agreed to reduce the expenditure.[13]

Charles Seely was elected as mayor of Lincoln by twelve votes to eight on 9 November 1840. His proposer, Thomas Newton, described Seely as a 'strenuous advocate of reform principles', 'a man of business habits, well known for his undeviating veracity and adherence to principle. Henry Blyth, seconding, said that he did so from a commercial point of view, 'mills were rising in every direction, and it was to such enterprising men as Mr Seely [they] had to look for the promotion of the welfare of the city.' Seely's remarks upon his election included a hope that the council should

---

[11] *Stamford Mercury*, 19 April 1839, 15 November 1839.
[12] Ibid., 20 December 1839.
[13] Ibid., 7 February 1840.

work with the lighting and paving commissioners to improve drainage and sewerage to rid the city of fever.[14]

One of Seely's earliest duties on becoming mayor was to head a corporate address to Queen Victoria upon the birth of her first child.[15] At the council meeting in February 1841 Seely suggested that the town clerk should complain to the General Post Office about the speed of their deliveries. He also started a debate as to whether he should allow 'wandering minstrels' to sing and play in the streets.[16] His concerns over excessive expenditure recurred over a bill of 17s. 6d. for mending windows at the Grammar School which he had refused to authorise without the consent of the council.[17] Seely's last council meeting was on 9 November 1841. He had not stood for re-election as a councillor and would never do so again. The same evening Seely attended the municipal festival at the Assembly Rooms. After his health had been given he gave a speech in which he prided himself on making the magistrates' court open to the public during the hearing of cases. His desire as head of the council had been to increase income as much as possible whilst decreasing expenditure. He had tried not to interfere with police matters and preferred to act with the consensus of the council rather than take on responsibility himself. As to a Tory charge of 'monopoly of power', he said that 'he was not a charity trustee – not a governor of Christ's Hospital – not an alderman – not even a simple town councillor now.' In challenging entrenched privileges and excessive expenditure in the 1830s and 1840s, Seely created the radical persona that he was to present to Lincoln's electors in subsequent parliamentary elections.

Charles Seely was involved publicly in two contentious issues in early Victorian Lincoln: railways and sanitation. Conflicting schemes for connecting Lincoln to the growing network of lines had been suggested. In 1844 he spoke at public meetings in Gainsborough and Lincoln.[18] He favoured George Hudson's plan to link Lincoln to his North Midland line at Swinton through Gainsborough and Doncaster. This would provide a shorter route to Manchester which was the largest buyer of ground wheat from

---

[14] Ibid., 13 November 1840.
[15] Ibid., 25 December 1840.
[16] Ibid., 5 February 1841.
[17] Ibid., 17 September 1841.
[18] Ibid., 19 & 26 April 1844.

Lincolnshire mills.[19] He also argued that Lincoln bought more and cheaper coal from the Swinton district than Wakefield, an alternative proposed route from Doncaster. Seely also supported Hudson's Nottingham to Lincoln line which was the first to reach the city in 1846.[20]

Though Lincoln escaped the national cholera epidemic of 1848-49, the council's sanitary committee had been alarmed enough to commission the civil engineer George Giles to draw up a report on the city's sanitation. In September 1849 he produced a 12,000-word report including proposals for action at a projected cost of almost £30,000. The council held two public meetings in the Cornhill, both chaired by the mayor James Snow, a surgeon. At the first, on 24 January 1850, Seely suggested that some common land could be sold in order to pay for sewerage. The ensuing outcry obliged the mayor to dissolve the meeting. Seely spoke again at the second meeting on 27 May 1850 and proposed a resolution in favour of the council's recommendation to adopt the Giles report. He was barracked for suggesting that money should be spent improving the health of the working class. Dirt was, to his mind, intimately connected to disease, immorality and crime. He thought that the sale of the manure removed from the city would defray running expenses. His proposal to sell 72 acres of Lincoln's South Common to pay for the main sewerage caused uproar as opponents tried to mount the stage. A proposal to reject the plan was carried amidst uproar and Lincoln had to wait until 1881 for a sewerage scheme to be implemented.[21]

Charles Seely was approached to become a Liberal parliamentary candidate for Lincoln following the death of the alderman John Rudgard in November 1840. Having first declined the honour, Seely was persuaded to change his mind by a requisition signed by 203 of the city's freemen and electors. In his initial address he supported the right of all householders to possess the vote but did not feel that 'the present state of political knowledge' justified manhood suffrage. He denied having ever been

---

[19] F. Hill, *Victorian Lincoln*, p. 106.
[20] Ibid., p. 109. See also N. R. Wright, *Lincolnshire Towns and Industry 1700-1914* (Lincoln, 1982) chapter 5.
[21] D. Mills, *Effluence and Influence: Public Health, Sewers and Politics in Lincoln, 1848-50* (Lincoln, 2015), pp. 108-12. See also pp. 103-5 for more on Charles Seely.

in favour of the total abolition of the Corn Laws but favoured a fixed duty rather than the sliding scale then existing. He would not, though, state a preferred amount of duty without further evidence.[22]

When Lincoln went to the poll in late 1841 Seely faced the two sitting members, the ultra-Tory Colonel Sibthorp and the reformer and successful novelist Sir Edward Bulwer. The Conservative William Collett, a banker and railway prospector, was the fourth candidate. Bulwer had lost popularity due to well-known marital difficulties, doubtful support for the Corn Laws and his opposition to changes in the 1834 Poor Law. He was beaten into second place by Collett as the Conservatives gained both Lincoln seats for the last time. Seely came in a distant fourth. His mother was said to have put up £3,000 towards his election expenses.[23]

In the election of 1847, held after the repeal of the Corn Laws and the split in the Conservatives, the same four candidates contested Lincoln. Collett's popularity had disappeared. He finished bottom of the poll whilst Seely took second place from Bulwer (now Bulwer-Lytton). Under their leader William Rudgard, the aggrieved Lincoln Whigs, who embodied the upper-middle classes of the city, attempted revenge on Seely by raising an election petition calling for his return to be declared void on the ground of corruption.

The select committee to examine the case began on 8 March 1848. Three of its five members could be classed as Liberals. Several Lincoln voters appeared as witnesses. The decisive evidence against Seely was given by John Shaw, a waterman. Before the election he had incurred a doctor's bill of 8s. 6d. which Seely had promised to pay. Though there was no mention then of Shaw promising to vote for Seely he received two payments after the election totalling forty shillings from Seely's clerk John Kealey. On 10 March the committee announced their resolution that Seely was not duly elected and that he was, through his agent Kealey, guilty of bribery though there was no evidence to show that Seely had any knowledge of the act. Seely's business partner T.M. Keyworth had stated in his evidence that Seely's 'crime' had been his rapid rise in status in Lincoln. It is hard to conclude that Seely had done

---

[22] *Stamford Mercury*, 25 December 1840.
[23] F. Hill, *Victorian Lincoln,* pp. 22-3. The return was Sibthorp 541, Collett 481, Bulwer, 443, Seely 340. *Stamford Mercury*, 2 July 1841.

anything worse than most candidates in contested elections and that he had simply made powerful enemies who were willing to spend heavily to exact revenge.[24]

Seely stood again for Lincoln in the General Election of 1852. Facing Colonel Sibthorp and the Whig George Heneage, he finished a well-beaten third. He had denied that four hundred men and boys had been released from Clayton and Shuttleworth to take part in the election. He also said that his mill workers were receiving the same wages as when flour was fetching a higher price and that his colliery manager had claimed an improvement in the conditions of the working class in Derbyshire. The voters of Lincoln were not so convinced by his belief in free trade.[25]

In his efforts to get into the House of Commons Seely had the support of the *Lincolnshire Times,* launched in January 1847 by Charles Pratt and William Gresham to promote the Liberal cause in Lincoln. Even before its first edition, it has been nicknamed 'Blunderbuss' by the Tory *Lincolnshire Chronicle.* It is not clear if Seely was a part-owner of the publication, but the *Chronicle* certainly thought it 'the property of the Seely clique' and it was edited for a time by 'Seely's agent' James Hitchins. The *Lincolnshire Times* passed out of its original owners' control in 1856. It had never had a large circulation – 300 per week in 1852 compared to the 1,540 for the *Lincolnshire Chronicle* and 12,060 for the *Stamford Mercury*.[26]

In February 1857 Seely made a further attempt at a parliamentary seat - this time in a by-election for Newport in the Isle of Wight. A newspaper correspondent described his appearance as 'of a spare, wiry figure ... His countenance is shrewd and clever; his forehead high, but rather retreating. Quick, restless eyes, and nervous lips show ... a clear, keen intellect, but great infirmity of purpose.'[27] In his hustings speech Seely professed support for the secret voting and wanted immediate abolition of church rates along with a reduction in government expenditure so that war taxation

---

[24] M. Acton, 'Beer & Bribery', *Lincolnshire Past & Present*, vol. 75 (2009), pp. 4-8.
[25] F. Hill, *Victorian Lincoln*, pp. 29-30.
[26] *Lincolnshire Chronicle,* 18 December 1846, 18 February 1848; D. Mills, *Effluence and Influence,* pp. 104-5; R.J. Olney, *Lincolnshire Politics* (1973), p. 85.
[27] *Isle of Wight Mercury*, 14 February 1857.

might be reduced. At the poll, though, he lost by 270 votes to 251 to the Conservative Robert Kennard.[28]

---

[28] *Hampshire Telegraph*, 14 February 1857.

III. An Entrepreneur

Piecing together the careers of nineteenth century businessmen is not an easy task, even in the case of a man like Charles Seely who was a conspicuous success, amassing a vast personal fortune. Business papers tended to be disposed of: not a single order book, balance sheet or purchase agreement relating to Seely's wide-ranging ventures has survived. What we can learn about Seely's commercial activities is to be found in contemporary newspapers and trade directories. Like other businessmen of the time, he favoured partnerships. These arrangements were often strengthened by marriage between family members of the business partners, but this was not the case with Seely. In his milling business in Lincoln Seely pooled resources with Thomas Michael Keyworth and John Coupland (who appears to have been a sleeping partner).[1] Initially Seely was involved in the day-to-day management of the mill, but, as his political career flourished, he stepped back. Eventually a manager was employed – for many years this was John Norton, 'a most honourable and upright man of business'.[2] In the early years of Seely's ventures into coal-mining in Derbyshire, the Keyworth family were also involved – T.M. Keyworth's younger brother John was a partner. When, in 1847, the manufacturers of agricultural machinery Clayton and Shuttleworth sought partners who were willing to assume unlimited liability for the business' debts, it was Seely and T.M. Keyworth who came forward, each securing a stake (probably 25 per cent) in the enterprise.[3] Later Seely moved to sole ownership of his businesses.

Skirted by malt houses, brew houses, mills and warehouses and with loaded barges regularly arriving and departing, Brayford Pool was the commercial centre of Lincoln. It was between Brayford Wharf and High Street that, in 1835, Keyworth and Seely erected their steam-powered mill. This was the second steam-

---

[1] Richard Coupland subsequently inherited his brother's share in the mill: *London Gazette*, 15 January 1861.
[2] *Lincolnshire Chronicle*, 22, 25 August 1882. Norton was connected with the mill for fifty seven years, retiring in 1880. He died suddenly from a cerebral haemorrhage whilst attending chapel, aged 73.
[3] R.C. Wheeler, 'The Rise of Clayton and Shuttleworth', *Lincolnshire History and Archaeology*, 47, p. 65.

powered mill to come into operation in Lincoln and became the heart of Keyworth and Seely's business operation – though they are also recorded as making use of two windmills.[4] Including fitting out, the steam mill cost about £28,000. Remarkably, within three years, this outlay had been covered by profits.[5] On occasion heavy rain led to flooding and brought the mill to a stop – but, doubtless to the owners' great relief, a storm which caused considerable damage in the city in January 1839 left the mill chimney standing.[6] Local people meanwhile were disappointed to note that the part of Brayford Pool in front of the mill into which hot water flowed did not freeze in winter and thereby limited the area on which they could skate.[7]

In the early years of the business Seely himself would travel by horse to market towns such as Boston and Sleaford to make arrangements to buy grain. He chose as his companion on these journeys Thomas Cooper, who was two years younger than him. A Gainsborough-born autodidact who wrote, with a strong radical flavour, the Lincoln column for the *Stamford Mercury*, Cooper shared Seely's interests in politics, literature and the human condition. It was a close friendship: these conversations were continued at Seely's house or during evening walks by the river Witham or across the fields at Canwick. When Seely had made his name in business and politics Cooper would often recall 'the one strong deep impression I caught of my friend's character – "This is the man whose purpose is formed and he will accomplish it"; and

---

[4] *Lincolnshire Chronicle,* 28 October 1887. C. Page, 'Mills in the Parish of St. Peter-at-Gowts' in A. Walker ed. *Lincoln's City Centre South of the River Witham* (Lincoln, 2015), p. 42 for the brief takeover of a steam mill in Salthouse Lane that had been run on co-operative lines by the Keyworth and Seely in the mid-1850s.

[5] *Lincolnshire Chronicle,* 28 October 1887.

[6] *Lincolnshire Notes & Queries,* VI, 1900-1, p. 134 for the story that, after he became mayor in November 1840, Seely was humorously known as 'the chimney mayor' after his seconder cited the tall mill chimney as adding to his suitability for the office.

[7] *Lincolnshire Chronicle,* 23 February 1855. The report concerns a near-drowning when the hot water temporarily stopped flowing and a man ventured onto the ice in front of the mill which gave way under 'so wreckless a freak.'

how completely that impression has been realised.'[8] The main market for Keyworth and Seely's flour was not in Lincoln, but in Manchester. John Kirk Keyworth, who also had a stake in the business, moved to Manchester to supervise the arrival and distribution of flour in the town.[9]

Their immediate and extensive profits enabled Keyworth and Seely to invest heavily in improving their operation. An adjoining yard was acquired in February 1847, and in November 1850 the mill was refitted with new machinery 'for the purpose of turning a finer flour'.[10] Though well-maintained, the flue collapsed in one of the three boilers in April 1856, 'producing continuous reports for about thirty seconds, the sounds being nearly equal to the report of cannon' and in April 1858 one of the now four boilers exploded, severely scalding a young engineer called Stephen Slater, who subsequently died of his injuries.[11] That summer new steam engines were installed – ever efficient, the owners ensured that the work was completed in only five weeks. The commercial success of Keyworth and Seely also owed much to their reputation for producing high-grade flour. Unlike many of their competitors, their flour, when tested, was never found to have been adulterated with salt or other substances.[12] Proudly, Keyworth and Seely flour left their mill in sacks stamped with their name. In his advertisements the Lincoln shopkeeper Henry Taylor declared that his flour was supplied by Keyworth & Seely 'which will be a sufficient guarantee of its superior quality'. [13]

With his involvement in Clayton and Shuttleworth's foundry, Seely was able to proclaim himself to be the largest employer in Lincoln. He stated that he employed on good wages about 400

---

[8] Thomas Cooper, *Life* (1872), p. 120. Cooper achieved great local notoriety for his contributions to the *Stamford Mercury*. See S. Roberts, *The Chartist Prisoners,* p.47.
[9] R.C. Wheeler 'The Rise of Clayton and Shuttleworth', p. 65. *Lincolnshire Chronicle,* 30 May 1868, for a court case brought by a rival miller concerning a discount Keyworth and Seely negotiated on the cost of transporting their flour to Manchester.
[10] *Lincolnshire Chronicle,* 29 November 1850.
[11] *Stamford Mercury,* 2 May 1856; ibid., 30 April 1858. The coroner raised the need for legislation to ensure the inspection of steam machinery.
[12] Ibid., 20 March 1857.
[13] *Lincolnshire Chronicle,* 6 May 1865. Ibid., 19 August 1884, for legal action taken by Keyworth and Seely against a shopkeeper who did not pay his bills.

hands in the city as iron founders, machine makers, millers, millwrights, joiners and labourers. Amongst his employees at the mill were John Harrison and Richard Thompson, both foreman, Henry Asman, a miller, John Pearson, a porter, Joseph Allott, 'the respected bookkeeper of Mr Charles Seely', and Gadsby and Rylett, both killed in accidents at the mill.[14] The local Tory editor did not care to hear Seely congratulating himself: 'We do hope Mr Seely shall not nauseate the public with vainglorious boastings about his men, his wages, his capital, his mill, his foundry and all his imaginary possessions.'[15]

Fatalities at the mill were rare, and were always attributed to bad luck rather than lack of care by the proprietors. When Richard Harvey, a foreman, was killed in November 1859 an eyewitness declared 'that no one was to blame' and the verdict of the coroner's jury was 'purely accidental'.[16] Keyworth and Seely, however, several times found themselves facing complaints for the excessive emission of smoke and soot. There were complaints in November 1848 and July 1855 and then, in October 1857, the city surveyor informed the lighting and paving commissioners, 'It has become the most intolerable nuisance the inhabitants of any place have to endure for, when the wind blows in one direction, the people have to endure the streets being covered with large black flakes and, as Messrs. Keyworth and Seely have four boilers, the fall of soot flakes at times is so great that those who are not eyewitnesses could not credit it.' It was said that women had to make use of umbrellas to protect their faces and dresses from the soot. The city surveyor attributed this nuisance 'upon good authority ... from the boilers and furnaces being supplied with inferior coal called ... "smudge" from Mr Seely's colliery.' In saying this, he was in fact in error: 'He presumed that his informant was correct but found that, for five or six years past, no "smudge" from Mr Seely's colliery had been consumed at the mill and the article consumed was "slack" from the Yorkshire collieries, which was of inferior quality to the coal consumed in other mills in the city.' Seely said the matter should be taken up with John Norton and was accused of 'throwing the

---

[14] Ibid., 24 September 1852. It was reported that Seely sent Allot to interview a voter who it was believed had been bribed to vote for the Tory candidates Sibthorp and Heneage; the voter was 'very indignant' at receiving this approach.
[15] Ibid., 19 March 1852.
[16] *Stamford Mercury,* 25 November 1859.

cold shoulder on complaints'; but, when a letter from the lighting and paving commissioners, was sent directly to him, improvements were made to the furnace.[17] At a cost of only six shillings the outcome was that 'there has not been the slightest fall of soot ... before the soot fell as thickly as snow in a snowstorm.'[18]

The steam mill had an imposing neighbour – the station, offices and coal depots of the Great Northern Railway Company. Keyworth and Seely were significant customers of the GNR, but, on occasion, relations became strained. For several months over winter 1867-8 a dispute rumbled on over access to a siding, which the mill had used for many years. The cause, Norton observed, was the GNR 'being determined to have their own way as usual'.[19] What he requested was not exclusive use of the siding for the mill but priority of use. The town clerk made clear that he agreed with Norton that the GNR was being highhanded and the dispute was declared to be 'amicably settled.'[20] The mill secured priority use.

With the mill making handsome profits year-on-year, Keyworth and Seely began to look at involving themselves in new ventures. In 1842 Nathaniel Clayton and Joseph Shuttleworth had built an iron foundry on one side of the dock basin at Stamp End and had begun to produce girders and pipes. Three years later they made a great technological and commercial breakthrough by unveiling a portable steam engine which could be used to drive a threshing machine. With the withdrawal of a partner who was providing capital in April 1847, Clayton and Shuttleworth sought new men to join the partnership. In return for equal stakes in the business with its founders, Keyworth and Seely provided the financial guarantees that enabled expansion to take place. This expansion was impressive. In less than a decade the workforce of 60 grew to 700, with a wage bill in excess of £17,000; and the buildings sprawled across eight acres.[21] At one point it was reported that Keyworth and Seely were 'in treaty for the purchase of the piece of land on the east side of the basin forming the eastern

---

[17] *Lincolnshire Chronicle*, 21 November 1848, 6 July 1855, 9 October 1857; *Stamford Mercury*, 9 October 1857.
[18] Ibid., 27 November 1857.
[19] Ibid., 20 December 1867.
[20] Ibid., 6 March 1868.
[21] *Lincolnshire Chronicle*, 14 July 1854 for a detailed description and an engraving of the Stamp End Works.

boundary of their iron foundry with the purpose of erecting a cotton factory.'[22] There was, however, to be no cotton factory. Whilst Keyworth had the time to involve himself in the management of the business, Seely did not. Taking his share of ever-increasing profits but not actually investing any capital eventually led to great ill feeling between Seely and Clayton and Shuttleworth. Seely believed he was simply adhering to the original agreement, and, when he was bought out in April 1869, it was amidst great rancour. 'Now you need never speak to me again', were said to be Clayton's words to Seely as he handed over the cheque.[23]

When he was in partnership with Seely in Lincoln in the late 1820s as a bone grinder, miller and coal merchant, John Coupland had also begun to develop mining interests in Derbyshire. He formed partnerships with Humphrey Goodwin and then with William Goodwin to operate the collieries at Birchwood and Cotes Park. This arrangement came to an end in October 1848. When Seely became involved is far from clear. It seems that John Kirk Keyworth – the younger of the brothers – formed a partnership with Coupland, who contributed the bulk of the capital. Coupland sank a new shaft which he named after Skellingthorpe, where his country house was located. These operations sought to extract anthracite, the most financially rewarding type of coal. About 200 men and boys were employed. Probably Seely did not become involved until, with the venture not turning out to be profitable, he bought out Coupland. He formed a partnership with Keyworth, which was dissolved in November 1855.[24] This did not mean the end of partnerships for Seely coal mining operations – Nathaniel Clayton, for example, later become involved but almost certainly as a sleeping partner.[25]

The miners who worked for Seely rarely saw him. He employed an agent to take care of the management of the pits. His chosen man was Joseph Radford, an experienced miner who, he calculated, his employees would respect and accept instructions from. When Seely did make an appearance, he sought to present

---

[22] Ibid., 17 December 1852.
[23] F. Hill, *Victorian Lincoln*, p. 189. Also see ibid., pp. 29, pp. 121-2; *Lincolnshire Chronicle*, 16 April 1869.
[24] *London Gazette*, 15 January 1861. Nineteenth century partnership dissolution statements often raise more questions than they answer.
[25] Ibid., 18 November 1870

himself as being on the side of his employees. Addressing 600 of his men at a dinner to mark the retirement of Radford in August 1868, he did more than pay tribute to a reliable agent:

'If anything occurred at the pits, he knew they used not to trouble their heads if Mr Radford was there, as all would be right ... To him it seemed that colliers were hardly dealt with in the opinion of the public. There were three dangerous occupations in England viz. those of soldiers, sailors and colliers ... He believed that men doing their duty as colliers deserved as much honour as soldiers and sailors (Loud cheers) ... He was an advocate of perfect independence and equality between masters and men. He had certain coal to get and they had certain strong arms to get it with ... There had been a great deal said about trade unions and freedom of labour and, while he did not fear in the least the effects of unions, he was partial to freedom of labour. He very much preferred freedom of labour, and he was of the opinion that, by that arrangement men, would get better wages.'[26]

Seely was never slow in pointing out that his investments in the collieries provided employment for hundreds of men. He would, however, have undoubtedly seen the advance of unionization as a threat to his control over his workforce and to his profits. Established in 1863, the Derbyshire and Nottinghamshire Miners' Association, had by this time recruited several thousand members as it campaigned for fewer hundredweights to the ton and shorter days. In truth Seely had little understanding of the lives of these men. He never witnessed the accidents which led to injury and death.[27] He could not understand why working conditions sometimes compelled his men to absent themselves from work. He responded to demands for higher wages by recourse to the law. 'The court was crowded with turnouts from Seely's colliery', it was reported when ten men appeared before the magistrates in January 1875, charged with walking out.[28]

By 1880 Seely had acquired seven collieries. In Derbyshire these were Birchwood, Shady and Tibshelf, located to the north-

---

[26] *Derby Mercury,* 12 August 1868.
[27] Ibid., 15 July 1857, *Derby Advertiser,* 20 November 1861, 9 February 1870 for accidents in pits owned by Seely which resulted in death and serious injury.
[28] *Derby Mercury,* 20 January 1875. Unsurprisingly the magistrates decided that the walk-out was illegal and ordered the ten men to pay 10s compensation, 7s 6d costs and return to work.

east of Alfreton; and in Nottinghamshire they were Bulwell, Cindermill, Kimberley and Newcastle. The expansion of Seely's mining interests into Nottinghamshire had got underway when he formed an association with Thomas North of the long-established Babbington Coal Company, and in 1859 sank shafts at Kimberley. Most of the men at this colliery did not belong to the union, and a campaign was launched to recruit them. Speakers at public meetings declared that the miners at Kimberley were 'held in bonds and had to bear burdens which were intolerable' and were 'tyrannised over by one master in particular.'[29] North was forbearing towards trade unions and these comments could conceivably refer to Seely. North died in February 1868, with considerable debts. Within a few years, his collieries were in Seely's possession. Seely built terraced housing to accommodate his employees. It was a part of his strategy to appear an owner who placed the miners' interests on the same level as his own.

'Seely's mill' – as it was always known to local people – was sold in summer 1891 to the Great Northern Railway Company, which was seeking to extend its warehouses and sidings. The business then moved to new premises at Sleaford, taking over a large steam mill previously occupied by Kirk and Perry.[30] This was a decision made by Seely's successors: with grain imports from Canada arriving to be milled in Hull, it is not implausible to suggest that Seely's instincts would have led him to wind up the business. The Seely family sold their coal investments in Derbyshire in the 1930s to the Sheepbridge Coal and Iron Company. Through the Babbington Coal Company – three of whose five directors were family members – they remained pit proprietors in Nottinghamshire until nationalisation in 1947.

There is an interesting coda to the story of Seely's business career. He was said to have been known as 'Pigs' on account of the fact that, in 1850, he signed a contract of fifty years' duration to supply the Admiralty with pig iron for use as ballast from the iron foundry at Stamp End and insisted on upholding this even when the Royal Navy, with its new steamships, no longer had a need for this

---

[29] *Nottingham Journal,* 12 April 1867, 14 July 1874.
[30] *Stamford Mercury,* 10 July 1891.

material.[31] This may well seem like the behaviour of a man who believed in enforcing contracts, but there is no evidence to support the assertion.[32]

From his interests in milling, the manufacture of agricultural machinery and coal mining, Charles Seely accumulated great wealth – much of which he invested in land assets. This did not happen because of his technological skills. Seely never applied for a patent for improvements in manufacturing – indeed on one occasion he was actually accused of infringing a patent.[33] Nor could it be said that Seely demonstrated a particular talent for marketing. He did not, as other manufacturers did, use newspapers to promote his business successes – there were no engravings or descriptions of his mill, let alone advertisements for his flour. Seely certainly did benefit from cheap, non-unionized labour; but his success surely owed much to his own ambition and drive. Seely was a single-minded and unyielding businessman: he pursued bakers for the money they owed him, he asserted what he saw as his rights against the claims of Nathaniel Clayton and Joseph Shuttleworth and he resorted to the law to deal with colliers who walked out to secure higher pay. Clearly he also had an eye for a business opportunity – Clayton and Shuttleworth had run out of money when he stepped in and the collieries owned by Coupland were making loses when he bought them out. Seely negotiated contracts that, though they might at first make a loss, he believed would become profitable in the long term. Having perhaps endured an initial loss and taken the risk that his forecasts of changes in conditions might not prove to be correct, he believed that, once a contract became profitable, he had every right to rigidly enforce it.[34] The success that Seely encountered in his commercial ventures clearly owed a great deal to the fact that he was not just an astute but also a hard-nosed businessman.

---

[31] B. Scott, *Galloper Jack: The Remarkable Story of a Man who Rode a Real War Horse* (2012), pp. 14-15.
[32] The reason for Seely becoming known as 'Pigs' is made clear in chapter IV.
[33] *Stamford Mercury*, 11 July 1856.
[34] We are grateful to Rob Wheeler for this observation.

IV. 'The Naval Reformer'

At the end of 1861 Charles Seely finally managed to manoeuvre himself into House of Commons. Lined up by the Liberal powerbrokers in Lincoln as their first preference to contest the next election was the barrister John Hinde Palmer, but he was out of the country when the sitting MP Gervaise Sibthorp died in October 1861. And so it was that one month later, without opposition, 'Charles Seely slipped in', as one wag declared at a public meeting.[1] Seely presented himself as an 'independent radical', called for the widening of the borough franchise and for the abolition of church rates and 'resisted the blandishments of Cabinet ministers', preferring instead to entertain the celebrated Richard Cobden at his country house on the Isle of Wight.[2] This, however, did not stop him seeing merits in Palmerstonianism. When the Prime Minister decided he could do nothing but watch the occupation of Denmark by Prussia and Austria in spring 1864, Seely made clear his approval of non-intervention.

Seely was fifty eight when he realised his long-held ambition. He was to be returned on another four occasions by the electors of Lincoln, topping the poll twice. The town clerk J.W. Tweed was recruited as his long serving agent. Seely's dogged determination in the House of Commons to expose what he saw as the inefficiency and profligacy of the Board of Admiralty resulted in him being referred to in the newspapers as 'the naval reformer'. In Lincoln the Liberals expressed their pride in his performance, and even the Tories, whose dislike of Seely was deeply entrenched, grudgingly conceded that his parliamentary efforts were worthwhile – though a former employee accused him of seeking to reduce wages in the naval dock yards to the level they were at Stamp End.[3] With regular reports in the press of his speeches in the House of Commons, Seely was able in 1865 to sidestep without much

---

[1] *Lincolnshire Chronicle,* 14 February 1862. Also see ibid., 20 January, 10 February 1860. Doubting their chances of success, the Tories did not bring forward a candidate at the by election.
[2] Ibid., 7 July 1865.
[3] Ibid., 24 June 1865.

commotion his own declaration that MPs should address their constituents at the beginning of each year.[4]

Seely entered the House of Commons with every intention of making his mark. Seeing himself as a businessman in politics, he intended to see the principles that enabled him to operate his own ventures so successfully applied to government departments. After considering the War Office, he decided that the Board of Admiralty would be the focus of his attention. The Board of Admiralty was responsible for the running and operations of the Royal Navy. It was a big spender. When Seely was elected to the House of Commons, the Cabinet position of First Lord of the Admiralty was held by the Duke of Somerset. In succession he was followed by Sir John Pakington (1866-7), H.T.L. Corry (1867), Hugh Childers (1868-71), George Goschen (1871-4), George Ward Hunt (1874-7) and W.H. Smith (1877-80). All of these men sat in the House of Commons. The First Lord of the Admiralty was assisted by four Naval Lords, a Civil Lord and a financial secretary.

Each year when the naval estimates came up for debate, Seely drew attention to what he regarded as wasteful spending. His favourite method of exposing profligacy was to compare costs in naval dockyards with those in private dockyards. His speeches were lengthy and full of figures. To provide him with information, this very thorough man employed secretaries and visited the naval dockyards at Portsmouth and Chatham. Seely began his campaign with the cost of protecting the naval dockyards, declaring the figure of £38,450 allocated for 1864 as 'preposterously high'.[5] He found the practice of searching men as they left at the end of each day not only costly but 'degrading'.[6] In Seely's opinion the employment of better managers and better relations with the men in the naval dockyards would make this unnecessary. Another issue that perplexed Seely was the sums being paid by the Admiralty for iron forgings. These cost 13s. 8d. per cwt. – yet the foundry at Stamp End could produce them at 6s. 9d. per cwt. He informed MPs that what could have been obtained for £19,718 had in fact cost £39,540. But this wasn't all. Seely discovered that ships were being repaired at a cost greater than if they had been replaced with new

---

[4] Ibid., 20 January 1865.
[5] *Hansard*, vol. 173, col. 1968.
[6] Ibid., vol. 178, col. 952.

ships. Amongst the examples he gave was the 17-gun *Lyra* which had been repaired at a cost of £17,653 whereas a replacement would have cost £16,964. It was clear to Seely that men with experience in business rather than naval officers should be appointed as managers in the dockyards: 'there were not placed at the head of each department in our dockyards men who knew the value of work.'[7]

These speeches were made by Seely in 1864-5. Amongst the MPs who backed him was John Bright.[8] The Civil Lord Hugh Childers and the financial secretary Lord Clarence Paget replied. Seely was informed that the iron forgings used in the naval dockyards were of superior quality; that ships took longer to build than repair; and that naval officers, with their authority and knowledge, were best suited for managing the dockyards. With Palmerston appearing in the House of Commons to make clear his opposition, a motion introduced by Seely to bring in commercial men was defeated by 60 votes to 33. However, Childers was a supporter of economy and he undertook to provide clearer statements about expenditure in the dockyards and invited Seely for discussions at the Admiralty.

In summer 1865 Seely again sought to be returned to the House of Commons, along with a second Liberal candidate, the country gentleman Edward Heneage. His long-time supporters Clayton and Shuttleworth were on the platform and, over an hour and a half, Seely set out what being an 'independent radical' entailed: support for extending the vote along the lines advocated by P.J. Locke King and Edward Baines, for the re-distribution of seats, for alterations to the oaths that Catholic MPs so objected to, for the abolition of church rates and for a peaceful foreign policy.[9] To these Seely added his personal commitments to spurning offers of

---

[7] Ibid., vol. 173, col. 1968.
[8] Ibid., vol. 180, col. 389. Bright observed that, compared to his own earlier criticisms of the Board, Seely's 'capable' interventions amounted to 'a mere whisper of discontent.'
[9] MP for East Surrey P.J. Locke King made several attempts during the 1850s to extend the county franchise. MP for Leeds and proprietor of the *Leeds Mercury*, Edward Baines introduced bills to introduce a borough franchise at a lower yearly rental of £6 in 1861 and 1865. Seely strongly deplored the bombardment by the Royal Navy of Kagoshima in Japan in August 1863 following the murder of a British trader.

parliamentary patronage and to the paying of good wages. Seely topped the poll, with Heneage also elected; the Tory candidate John Bramley Moore, a Liverpool ship owner, trailed well behind.[10] In what had become a Lincoln custom, there was an outbreak of stone throwing between rival supporters after the result had been declared.

It was business as usual for Seely when he returned to the House of Commons. To him it seemed that 'the Admiralty had ... gone from bad to worse.'[11] He contrasted the costs of ships of about the same tonnage built in private yards with those built in naval yards – he observed that the figure for *Warrior* built by a private company on the Thames was £360,995 whilst that for the *Achilles* built by the Admiralty at Chatham was £472,790. He questioned the price of anchors, claiming that, since 1847, the supplier used by the Admiralty had been paid £170,000 above the prices that would have been charged by other manufacturers. With regard to Greenwich Hospital, he wanted to know what a captain-superintendent and his two lieutenants, earning respectively £1,280 and £800 a year, actually did and why eighteen police constables were needed when twenty four were sufficient for Lincoln. He also wondered why there were 190 admirals on the active and retired list, two for every ship in commission in his calculation. Seely's usual method of operation was to withdraw his motions, satisfied that he had got the financial secretary or the First Lord to respond. His calculations might be questioned, but the financial secretary Clarence Paget always made sure he praised Seely for his sharp eye and invited him for further discussions at the Admiralty.

In discovering that the Board of Admiralty had purchased iron ballast – known as 'pigs' – to be put down as road surfacing and workshop flooring in naval dockyards, Seely knew that he had found the issue on which to hang his arguments about wasteful expenditure. He told the story with great satisfaction at a public meeting in Lincoln in January 1867:

'I ... pointed out that there was some iron ballast, familiarly called pigs, and I think it probable these pigs will give a squeak when Parliament meets again. I ventured to say that these pigs were worth £150,000 or £160,000 and that they were employed for

---

[10] Seely 878; Heneage 870; Bramley Moore 765.
[11] *Hansard,* vol. 182, col. 333.

purposes in many cases useless and in some cases worse than useless. I am speaking to men who have some practical knowledge of the matter and they will know whether I am right. I instanced the case of the smithies - and there are men here who work in smithies - and I was told that it was a blunder to put down iron for floors of smithies as it was too hot in summer and too cold in winter and, if the Admiralty offered to put down for nothing these pigs at Stamp End, we would not have them. At a most modest estimate there is £150,000 to £160,000 wasted in this atrocious manner. If they knew the value of this iron, really it is criminal; if they did not know why, they are fools. I dislike excessively to see the public money squandered in this way. I am told that besides the 35,000 tons included in the return they gave me, there is a great quantity of these pigs to be found in Bermuda and various parts of the world, lying in ships bottoms in ordinary; and the *United Services Gazette,* some three or four weeks ago, stated that they believed the quantity would be nearly double. If so, there would be about 60,000 or 70,000 tons, the value of which would be something like £300,000, entailing a loss of £9,000 a year at only three per cent interest, the rate at which government can borrow money.'[12]

After investigating Seely's claims, the First Lord Sir John Pakington had conceded that he was correct in what he said. Though the ballast had been bought in the early part of the century, it was worth selling - Seely mischievously made an offer of £100,000.[13] The 'startled' newspapers declared that the country was 'greatly indebted' to Seely.[14] Even *Punch* commented with respect: 'These pigs of iron may be regarded as a sort of prize pigs. After the name of their discoverer, they have been denominated "Mr Seely's pigs". For this the nation should be grateful to Mr Seely who has saved so much of its bacon.'[15] In Lincoln Seely's re-election was seen as certain and no Tory candidate made an appearance in November 1868. A bullish Seely turned up anyway to proclaim his support for extending the scope of the previous

---

[12] *Lincolnshire Chronicle,* 25 January 1867.
[13] The pigs were deemed to be worth £3-4 a ton. A number of examples were put on show at a meeting or ironmongers in Birmingham. It is not clear how the Board of Admiralty eventually disposed of the iron ballast.
[14] *Cambridge Independent Press,* 9 March 1867.
[15] *Punch,* 23 March 1867.

year's Reform Act, for secret voting and for the re-distribution of seats.

Up until the early 1870s Seely continued 'hammering away at the Admiralty'.[16] There were his familiar motions concerning the costs of repairing and building ships, the prices being paid for anchors, the inadequacies of the management of naval yards – he reported that on a visit to one yard 'greater skulking and greater waste he had never seen in his life' - and the cost and management of Greenwich Hospital.[17] Unsurprisingly for a businessman who embraced technical improvements, Seely also became an advocate of building ships with revolving gun turrets.[18]

The necessity for reform of the Board of Admiralty was very evident to Gladstone's Liberal government, which came into office, with Hugh Childers as First Lord, in December 1868. By order-in-council in January 1869, the Naval Lords were reduced in number from four to three and ceased to jointly supervise affairs with individual responsibilities specified instead. With each man getting on with his own work, the number and length of meetings was greatly reduced - the Board, which had previously convened for hours each day, met briefly on only thirty three occasions in 1870. There was to be greater financial supervision and a design committee comprising of naval officers and technical experts was set up. The number of clerks was also brought down, with lower-paid writers taking on some of their duties.[19] Whilst Seely welcomed improvements in the system of accounting and a reduction in the number of dockyards, he continued to press for men with business experience to be recruited and for the Board, with too many 'incompetent' people working to it, to be abolished.[20] 'The thing is monstrous and ridiculous', he declared.[21] His strong-worded speeches certainly caused offence. The Board was never going to agree to naval officers being replaced in the yards, and Seely's

---

[16] *Hansard,* vol. 214, col. 963.
[17] Ibid., vol. 207, col. 1462.
[18] Instead of rows of guns on each side, turret ships had a rotating gun turret. The Royal Navy's first sea-going turret ship was completed in 1869.
[19] See C.I. Hamilton, *The Making of the Modern Admiralty: British Naval Policy 1805-1927* (Cambridge, 2011), pp. 153-60.
[20] *Hansard,* vol. 207, col. 1446.
[21] Ibid., vol. 207, col. 1460.

motion in February 1873, for a Secretary of State to administer the Admiralty was defeated by 114 votes to 13.

The acrimonious rupture with his business partners Clayton and Shuttleworth had repercussions for Seely's political operations in Lincoln. The two men had long been influential promoters of Seely's parliamentary ambitions and now they withdrew their support completely. When, in August 1870, Seely visited Lincoln, Clayton and Shuttleworth were noticeable by their absence from a dinner he gave for his supporters – and the next day he did not attend a lunch they put on at Stamp End. It was reported that they intended to oust Seely. 'I have just heard that Mr Seely is to go and the next candidate is to be moulded at Stamp End', an amused correspondent observed.[22] If there was a plan for either Clayton or Shuttleworth to come forward, it did not come to fruition and, at the beginning of 1874, Seely again presented himself to the electors of Lincoln. With Palmer, he addressed two meetings. Describing himself – rather inaccurately – as 'a small landed proprietor', he spoke at length about his support for extending the vote to agricultural labourers and for greater fairness in land tenure for small farmers.[23] So a reformer still; but Seely also remembered to remind the people that he had remained loyal to them and they should remain loyal to him. It was not the independently-minded Seely, who was able to interpret almost anything he endorsed as Liberalism, but Palmer, who did not hide his admiration for the despised Gladstone, that the Lincoln Tories saw as their real enemy. They sought to remove him by bringing forward the youthful Edward Chaplin, whose experience did not extend much beyond fox hunting. Along with Seely, Chaplin was returned – over the next six years he was not to make a single intervention in parliamentary debates. Clayton – though not Shuttleworth – announced that he would vote for Seely. For his troubles he received a 'severe' blow on the chest from a stone thrown during a riot that preceded polling day.[24]

As ever, Seely returned to the House of Commons his own man. He remained silent on the Liberal touchstone of temperance and was not necessarily willing to fall in behind Gladstone. 'Fancy

---

[22] *Lincolnshire Chronicle*, 12 August 1870.
[23] *Lincoln Gazette*, 31 January 1874.
[24] *Lincolnshire Chronicle*, 6 February 1874.

Lincoln without beer ... The thought is too much for me', a satirist had Seely saying in a speech before he 'sank exhausted and a glass of beer was brought to him.'[25] He returned, of course, to naval matters, raising questions about the designs of ships, the narrow recruitment of engineers and expenditure. He spoke out in support of securing a penny rate for postcards sent to Europe and the United States. He also took a leading part in seeking to limit the control that landowners exerted over tenant farmers. Seely believed that it was unjust that departing tenants could not be compensated for improving the soil and drainage and erecting new buildings. He introduced a motion to provide compensation; Disraeli described Seely's speech as 'extremely sensible' but 'abstract' and 'vague'.[26] The outcome was government legislation. The Agricultural Holdings Act of 1875, however, did not incorporate Seely's amendment that a tenant farmer should be able to remain for two months after giving notice to quit and, most importantly, did not make compensation compulsory. Landowners did not apply the legislation and tenant farmers had to wait until 1883 to be legally entitled to compensation. In August 1879 Seely asked a question about money owed by the India Office to the War Office. It proved to be his last parliamentary intervention.

In Lincoln Seely continued to be a generous benefactor to charitable institutions. In 1878 he donated £200 to the dispensary and £1000 to the hospital. Although he was again returned in April 1880, disillusionment with their maverick MP was growing in the ranks of the Liberal Association. Increasingly he began to stay away from the House of Commons, but this was not the only cause for concern. In an era of the National Liberal Federation and the progressive Liberalism of Joseph Chamberlain, Seely seemed a figure from an earlier generation. He still made brief visits to Lincoln, but did not conceal his own disillusionment. The Tory MP for South Lincolnshire J.C. Lawrence praised a 'wonderful' speech he made during a visit to his constituency and hoped 'they would hear more of those fine Conservative maxims such as Mr Seely treated his Liberal friends to the last time he was in Lincoln.[27] Though in his early eighties, Seely had no desire to retire and he

---

[25] Ibid, 13 September 1877.
[26] *Hansard*, vol. 220, cols. 205-7.
[27] *Lincolnshire Chronicle,* 2 February 1883.

still called himself a Liberal. Waiting in the wings, however, was a ready-made alternative, over thirty years younger, energetic and much more in tune with the views of the Liberal Association. This was the ironmaster Joseph Ruston, who was to become Seely's successor.

V. At Home

Charles Seely became the father of six children and the owner of three country houses. He was a man who knew well the comforts that family life and wealth could bring. For the early part of their marriage, Charles and Mary Seely lived at 8 James Street in Lincoln. Of the five children born when they lived in the city, two of them Charles (b. 1832) and John (b. 1839) died when they were a few months old. A second son, also called Charles, arrived in August 1833 and, in June 1836 and March 1837, he acquired two sisters Mary and Frances. The houses in James Street, overlooked by the cathedral and with gardens, were occupied by gentlemen. In 1841 the domestic needs of the Seely family were catered for by four servants.

A successful and wealthy man by the time he reached forty, Seely decided that it was time to show this. In September 1844 he sold 8 St. James Street to his partner T.M. Keyworth, and purchased a small country house in Heighington, four miles from Lincoln. It seems that Seely bought the house after it had been rented out for a number of years by the widow of its former occupant, Thomas Dyson Holland. This 'most desirable residence' provided 'every accommodation which can be required by a family': a dining room (24'x18'), a drawing room (22'x10'), a breakfast room, nine bedrooms, a 'capacious' kitchen, 'neatly fitted-up' sculleries, 'capital' cellars, a 'very tastefully laid-out' garden, an orchard and a gardener's cottage. It suited the needs of a rising manufacturer and politician very well; had he been so inclined, it also offered Seely the opportunity 'to participate in the sports afforded by the celebrated hunting establishment of Sir Richard Sutton.'[1] One month after their arrival at Heighington, in October 1844, the Seelys' final child Jane arrived.

Seely would travel each day from his country house by carriage into Lincoln, with the exception of during election contests when,

---

[1] *Lincolnshire Chronicle*, 10 February 1837, 28 February 1840. Sir Richard Sutton was master of the Burton foxhounds, two of which he presented to Queen Victoria in 1838. On his estate in Norfolk 'in little more than three days' Sutton and ' a small party of friends' shot 1,313 pheasants and 'an immense quantity' of hares, rabbits, partridges and woodcocks. (Ibid., 22 February 1839).

needing to be readily available, he stayed at a relative's house or a hotel. On one occasion, without invitation, his political rivals visited him at home. Hatching a plan in an inn to mischievously seek Seely's support for the Whig Henry Welbourne Jones in July 1845, they were told by his servants that Seely only saw visitors by appointment and were turned away. Seely, however, decided to play along and admitted them and 'at length port and sherry, with a due supply of substantials, were forthcoming and the jolly dogs had a delightful fuddle ... We have not learned whether they obtained a promise for Mr Jones or not.'[2]

In 1851 Seely and his wife lived at Heighington with their daughters Mary, Frances and Jane, Charles having left the family home. There were two servants. By 1861 Mary was married, leaving Frances and Jane at home. There were four servants: Alice Stafford McKenzie, aged 44 and unmarried, was cook and housekeeper and Martha Taylor, Mary Buller and Mary Goodwin were housemaids. McKenzie had been born in Newark, and the three housemaids in Lincoln. A decade later Taylor was still working for the Seely family, at their house in London.

Established in their country house, Charles and Mary Seely became leading figures in Lincolnshire society. Seely was appointed, at the end of 1859, a deputy lieutenant of the county. The arrival of Seely and his wife at Heighington would be reported in the county newspaper, and their names would appear in the lists of attendees at balls for the county elite. The couple associated themselves with philanthropic and charitable causes. In early 1859 Seely, 'with his customary liberality', provided funds for the building of a Methodist school in Lincoln, and he also supported the county hospital – donating £100 in June 1860 – and the Mechanics Institute. His wife meanwhile became patroness of various charitable balls: in November 1860 a ball at the assembly rooms to obtain funds for the dispensary raised £127. 7s. 7d.[3]

In early 1868 it was reported that Seely was selling Heighington. His agent anxiously denied that this was a first step in severing links with Lincoln.[4] The house now passed into the hands

---

[2] Ibid., 11 July 1845.
[3] Ibid., 31 December 1858, 14 January, 4 February, 30 September, 7 October 1859, 8 June, 2 November, 30 November 1860.
[4] Ibid., 2 May, 8 May 1868.

of Alfred Shuttleworth, the son of his partner in the iron foundry. Shuttleworth made significant alterations, and also brought in the in-demand landscape gardener Edward Milner, who had earlier laid out the gardens at his father's house, Hartsholme Hall.[5]

By this time Seely had been spending much of the year away from Heighington. When the House of Commons was sitting, he was to be found at 28 and then at 26 Prince's Gate, Westminster, and 7 Queen's Gate Gardens, Knightsbridge, before, in 1877, installing himself at Furzedown House in Tooting.[6] When not in London, he increasingly retreated to Brooke House in the Isle of Wight. The imposing five-storey houses of Prince's Gate and Queen's Gate Gardens had been built only a few years before Seely took up occupancy by, respectively, Charles Freake and Charles Aldin.[7] They were highly desirable addresses, and Seely's neighbours included not only fellow MPs but also army and naval officers, lawyers, baronets, even earls. When at home, Seely spent his days in a grand drawing room on the first floor. He was able to walk on mahogany floors and admire ornate plasterwork. These large houses required a large staff: in 1871 at 7 Queen's Gate Gardens, Seely was employing twelve servants, including a butler, a hall porter and three footmen. It was certainly all a long way from the life of a country gentleman in rural Lincolnshire.

An eighteenth century mansion set in 170 acres and overlooking Tooting Common, Furzedown House was seven miles from the House of Commons. Seely was able to afford the finest carriage horses to convey him there. His house in Heighington was

---

[5] On census night 1871 six servants, but no family, were recorded as being in residence; presumably alterations were underway. Edward Milner worked, in his early career, under the direction of Joseph Paxton and, as an independent landscape gardener, designed parks and gardens; amongst the latter was Highbury, the house of Joseph Chamberlain in Birmingham. Joseph Shuttleworth built Hartsholme Hall in 1862 on the edge of a lake earlier constructed by the Lincoln Water Company. It was demolished in 1951.

[6] From the electoral registers, it seems that for some years Seely was simultaneously renting 26 Prince's Gate and 7 Queens Gate Gardens. He continued to rent 26 Princes Gate for a year after he took up occupancy of Furzedown House. *Derby Mercury,* 23 November 1859 for a report that Seely was negotiating the purchase of Newstead Abbey after the death of its owner Thomas Wildman.

[7] Charles James Freake and Charles Aldin both rose from humble origins to become the builders of a number of garden squares in west London.

modest by comparison: at his Tooting mansion there were eighteen bedrooms, 'an unusually handsome set of reception rooms' and the 'beautifully-timbered' gardens included four 'fine' specimens of the uncommon Judas tree.[8] It seems likely that Seely acquired the mansion a number of years before he took up residence, during which time he added a large conservatory. For ten years prior to Seely's arrival the occupant of the house had been the Australian builder Philip Flower, who was responsible for erecting, at a cost of £15,000, St. Philip's Church in Battersea.[9] Almost certainly the Lincoln electors who had returned Seely to the House of Commons were unaware of the opulence of his London lifestyle.

'When I make my fortune, all this will be mine', Seely is reported to have declared when walking across the downs on the south-west coast the Isle of Wight in his teenage years.[10] He was staying with an aunt at Godshill during a period of recuperation from ill health. Whether or not he did utter this remark, Seely did, after purchasing Brooke House from the executors of James Howe in 1857, embark on a great expansion of his estates.[11] There are records of him buying land and farms over the next twenty years.[12] This required a considerable outlay of money; the purchase of the Bowcote and Brightstone estates from Sir John Simeon in 1873 cost Seely £85,930.[13] By this time Seely, who rode daily across his estates, had become known as the 'Squire of Brooke'. Located half a mile from the sea, Brooke House was enlarged and filled with fine furniture, old china and landscapes and seascapes by Copley Fielding, John Gilbert Edward Duncan and others. The gardens were remodelled, and the 'magnificent' vineries and hothouses 'gorgeous with the blooms of tropical plants' and 'hung with

---

[8] *Morning Post*, 23 June 1880; *Isle of Wight County Press*, 27 June 1885. Seely sought a buyer for the mansion in 1880, but one was not found and it remained in his son's hands. The grounds were sold off in the early twentieth century and in 1915 the mansion became a college for trainee teachers.

[9] *Clerkenwell News*, 14 July 1870.

[10] B. Scott, *Galloper Jack*, pp. 13-14.

[11] Brooke House had been in the possession of the Howe family since the late eighteenth century; James Howe died in April 1855, aged 77.

[12] Isle of Wight Record Office, 27A/3, 39A/3, 41A/6, 63A/1, 66A/1, 66A/22, 70A/3, 73A/8, 74A/1, 76A/1, 101A/9, 103A/4, 122A/1 112A/8.

[13] Sir John Simeon was MP for the Isle of Wight from 1847 to 1851 and again from 1865 to 1870.

festoons of grapes' were greatly admired by visitors.[14] On Seely's instructions there was to be no disturbing the tranquillity by the shooting of birds within earshot.

The Isle of Wight foxhounds would meet at Brooke House, sometimes enjoying oyster breakfasts before setting out. On one occasion, after being 'sumptuously entertained at breakfast', the huntsmen sent the brush of the fox they had killed to Seely's wife and daughters.[15] Seely also made his mansion available for meetings of the Philosophical and Scientific Society: in August 1867 the vicar of Brighstone gave a lecture on local geology.[16] The poor might not have toured the big house and its gardens, but, at the beginning of each year, Seely ordered his steward William Selby to provide each needy family in Brooke with 10lb of beef and suet, flour, sugar, tea and plums.[17] He certainly made clear his feelings about 'a core part of the village economy' - when he came across an illicit tub of brandy in his stables, he made 'a terrible-to-do ... say(ing) it was wrong to defraud the revenue ...'[18] Seely encouraged his tenants to collect for the Indian Mutiny Relief Fund in 1857 and they raised £10. 19s 9d. To this he added £25.[19]

Shipwrecks were not uncommon off the south-western coast of the Isle of Wight. In December 1859 the 'Marabita', a Maltese ship carrying oats from Marseilles to London, foundered off the coast of Chale Bay, with the loss of most of the crew. This event resulted in £700 being raised to pay for lifeboat stations at Brooke and Brighstone. In August 1860 'Dauntless' and 'Rescue' were launched from their respective stations. Seely contributed £100 to the costs of the Brooke station, and it was his wife who launched 'Dauntless'. With the provision several years later of £500 for the building of libraries in rural areas across the Isle of Wight, Seely's reputation as a progressive and philanthropist could not be in any

---

[14] *Isle of Wight Observer*, 14 July 1894, *Isle of Wight County Press*, 21 July 1900. For the gardeners and carpenters at work at Brooke House see D. Denaro Brooke-Smith & S. Mears, *Brook: A Village History*, pp. 155, 157.
[15] *Isle of Wight Mercury*, 31 October 1857.
[16] Ibid., 2 November 1867.
[17] *Isle of Wight Observer*, 4 January 1868, 1 January 1870.
[18] D. Denaro Brooke-Smith & S. Mears, *Brook: A Village History*, pp. 9-11.
[19] *Isle of Wight Mercury*, 31 October 1870.

doubt.[20] These sort of donations were stock-in-trade for Liberal businessmen, increasing the esteem in which they were held and strengthening their positions. Seely's upwards progress continued when he was appointed a deputy lieutenant of the Isle of Wight. The sums of money he gave away were very small for a man of his wealth, but, it should be remembered, that, without them, the opening of lifeboat stations or libraries in rural areas on the Isle of Wight would have been much longer delayed.

For a week in spring 1864 the attention of the nation focused on Brooke House. This was because Seely had welcomed into his mansion an illustrious guest with a huge following in Britain. Giuseppe Garibaldi was the hero of Italian unification in 1860. Seely was at Southampton docks to welcome him on his arrival on 3 April and the next day escorted him as he travelled by steamer and carriage to Brooke House for a week's recuperation before embarking on a provincial tour. The enthusiasm of the huge crowds that greeted Garibaldi at Southampton and of Seely was not shared by either Queen Victoria or Palmerston.[21] For them the idea of a revolutionary at large in the north stirring up the crowds and trying to drum up funds for the purchase of a warship was deeply unappealing. To ensure that Garibaldi left Britain as expeditiously as possible he was prevailed upon to abandon his planned tour with a reminder that his health would not stand up to it. After a week in the Isle of Wight, Garibaldi was successfully confined to London - staying in Seely's house in Prince's Gate - before departing for Capri.

Despite Garibaldi's early departure, Seely was able to bask in his own triumph. It was reported that he had 'won for himself golden opinions from everyone for the genial and generous welcome he has given the patriot.'[22] Seely had hired a steamer the 'Sapphire', which had been freshly painted in turquoise for the

---

[20] *Isle of Wight Observer,* 11 November 1876. Seely provided funds for the rebuilding of Brook Church after it had been destroyed by fire and also for the restoration of St Peter and St Paul Church after purchasing the Mottistone estate in 1861; additionally, shortly before his death, he put up the money for the building of a working men's club in Newport.

[21] R. Shannon, *Gladstone 1809-1865* (1982), pp. 501-4; M. Finn, *After Chartism: Class and Nation in English Radical Politics 1848-1874* (Cambridge, 1993), pp. 217-25.

[22] *Isle of Wight Times,* 14 April 1864.

occasion, to convey Garibaldi to the Isle of Wight and provided him with an excellent luncheon on board – though, unfortunately, his guest ate but little. On arrival at Cowes they had been met by a band, which struck up 'See The Conquering Hero Comes', and a carriage containing Mary and Charles Seely, and during the journey of fifteen miles to Brooke House had been accompanied by a considerable number of admirers. At Brooke House Mary Seely cut off a lock of Garibaldi's hair and Seely presented him with a supply of turnip seeds, which his guest later reported 'are growing magnificent.'[23] With Seely, Garibaldi had paid a visit to the most famous Lincolnshire-born man of the age, Alfred, Lord Tennyson. The poet-laureate had lived on the Isle of Wight at Farringdon House since 1853. Garibaldi had already planted an oak tree in the garden of Brooke House – which Seely christened the 'Tree of Liberty' – and now he put a Wellingtonia tree in the ground at Farringford.[24] For Mary Seely it was all too much. 'When, alas, you left me yesterday', she informed Garibaldi after he made a short second visit on his way home, 'my heart was full of anguish. I went to take another look at your small bed ... I stood contemplating it with a heavy heart when I noticed, near the bolster, the kerchief which you used ... what a comfort it was to me'.[25] Seely had the brass bedstead inscribed 'Garibaldi, 22nd of April 1864.' This enterprising man would surely have admired the entrepreneurial talents of his servants who marked Garibaldi's visit by selling hairs retrieved from a comb he had used and small bottles of water from his bath.

---

[23] D. Denaro Brooke-Smith & Susan Mears, *Brook: A Village History,* p. 118-9. The radical George Jacob Holyoake was a guest at the dinner on the evening of Garibaldi's arrival: see G.J. Holyoake, *Sixty Years of an Agitator's Life* (1892), II, pp. 119-24.
[24] J. Batchelor, *Tennyson* (2012), p. 259. The trees at Brooke House and at Farringford House have not survived, though saplings from the former can still be seen. We are grateful to Daphne Denaro Brooke-Smith for this information.
[25] Quoted in B. Scott, *Galloper Jack,* p. 16.

VI. Last Years

The story of Charles Seely is a striking example of the sort of upward mobility that was possible in Victorian England. Though not exactly of humble origins, he began life in relatively modest circumstances and, as a result of his investments in coal mining and land, ended it in possession of immense wealth. It was not, of course, a singular story. The architect of Seely's residence in Prince's Gate, Charles Freake, started out as a carpenter but died with personal wealth in excess of £700,000; and the MP James Morrison was the son of a publican who made his fortune in haberdashery, owning 10,000 acres of land at the time of his death.[1] From early on Seely was a businessman with an eye on making money, but his friend Thomas Cooper harboured ambitions that were equally strong. Cooper sought not wealth but acclaim as a poet. Seely was one of the first to hear about his intention to write a lengthy poem with the title of the *Purgatory of Suicides.* When it eventually appeared in 1845, his densely-packed 944-stanza poem established him as no more than a literary curiosity. In later life he survived on collections and sales of books at his lectures and Seely arranged for an annuity of £100 for his old friend.[2]

During the last few years of Seely's life one blow followed another. In summer 1884, after an illness extending over several months, Mary died at Furzedown House.[3] Her husband had reasoned that the best doctors were available in London, but she was buried in the Isle of Wight, at St. Mary's, Brooke. Cooper, himself widowed and regularly in touch with his friend by letter, wrote that Seely was 'now lonely, having ... lost the light of his life, whom I always deemed the most perfect woman in the world.'[4] Against his wishes Seely's parliamentary career also now came to an end. The Liberal Association had grown increasingly uncomfortable with his lack of support for Gladstone's administration.[5] It was

---

[1] We are grateful to Kathryn Rix for drawing our attention to James Morrison and also to another nineteenth century MP Joseph Locke, the son of a colliery manager who became a railway engineer and died with an estate worth £350,000.
[2] S. Roberts, *The Chartist Prisoners,* p. 140.
[3] *Lincolnshire Chronicle,* 26 August 1884.
[4] *Isle of Wight Observer,* 19 December 1885.
[5] *Stamford Mercury,* 17 November 1882; F. Hill, *Victorian Lincoln,* p. 194.

expected that Seely would make a fight of it, but, reminding the electors of his deep loyalties to Lincoln and Liberalism, he surprisingly announced his retirement.[6] Cooper was allowed to publicly object at 'what they have done' and a few members of the Liberal Association went with Seely but that was it.[7] He was never again to return to the city of his birth and which he had represented for almost a quarter of a century. It seemed an unusually meek acceptance of the situation from Seely, but that was far from the whole story.

As ever, Seely had a plan. He would remain in the House of Commons by supplanting the existing Liberal MP for the Isle of Wight. This was Evelyn Ashley, the son of Lord Shaftesbury who had been returned in 1880. Reports began to circulate that Ashley had given a pledge that he would stand aside if Seely ever wished to come forward as the Liberal nominee. Ashley firmly denied these and, in early November, a meeting was arranged between the two men in Newport. At this meeting Seely informed Ashley that he did not require the agreement of the Liberal Association and only needed to announce his withdrawal. Ashley refused to take such a step and Seely subsequently withdrew a promise to nominate him.[8] It was reported that Seely's son-in-law Colonel George Browne canvassed the tenants on the family estates in support of the Conservative candidate Sir Richard Webster.[9] When Webster defeated Ashley in December 1885, many Isle of Wight Liberals had no hesitation in blaming Seely.

Unsurprisingly the man who had long been accustomed to getting his way was unwilling to accept that his parliamentary career was over. He was still willing to listen to his admirers and to let them press his case. One such admirer discussed Seely's parliamentary resurrection whilst crossing from Portsmouth to Ryde and 'leaning on my arm, he walked the whole length of the pier'.[10] So, in early 1886, Seely's name was canvassed as the man to take on Webster. However, his attempt to oust Ashley, his opposition to Gladstone's Irish Home Rule Bill and his donation of £1000 to

---

[6] *Lincolnshire Chronicle,* 16 October, 27 October 1885. As a result of the Redistribution Act of 1885 Lincoln had been deprived of one MP.
[7] *Isle of Wight Observer,* 19 December 1885.
[8] Ibid., 5 December 1885.
[9] Ibid., 14 November 1885.
[10] *Isle of Wight County Press,* 29 October 1887.

'what he called the Unionist committee', were obstacles that were never going to be overcome.[11] The Isle of Wight Liberals chose instead Henry Stuart, who went down to a heavy defeat. Seely's small band of supporters - and doubtless Seely himself - believed he would have been returned.

Despite the destruction of his parliamentary ambitions, and at the end of 1886 sustaining injuries after being knocked down by a grocer's van in Newport, Seely had no intention of retiring from public life. By spring 1887 he was making his regular trips to Newport and that summer announced that, at a cost of £500, he would put on a public dinner to mark the golden jubilee of the Queen. When Victoria visited Newport on 22 July, Seely was amongst those presented to her, but the dinner did not go ahead. He decided it was too great an expense and the money was allocated instead to entertainment for the poor, the fox hunt and the Volunteers.[12]

The three daughters of Charles and Mary Seely married into the higher ranks of Isle of Wight society. Thomas Renwick, who married Mary in August 1860, was an Anglican clergyman, holding the livings of Mottistone and Shorwell. He died of a heart attack whilst out walking with friends in October 1874. Mary lived for another 33 years. Benjamin Temple Cotton, who married Frances in June 1861, took a degree from Oxford and owned an estate at Afton, near Freshwater, where he operated a number of stone quarries. In 1880 he stood unsuccessfully as the Conservative candidate for the Isle of Wight. Frances pre-deceased both her parents and her husband, dying of tuberculosis at the age of 32 in Cannes in November 1869. She was buried in Freshwater. Colonel Henry Browne, who married Jane in April 1862, was the son of an Isle of Wight J.P. and held the Victoria Cross after spiking a battery at Lucknow during the Indian Mutiny. He subsequently became a keen yachtsman.[13]

The ambitions of Charles and Mary Seely for their only surviving son were more than fulfilled. It was the younger Charles Seely who established the family dynasty in business and politics.

---

[11] Ibid.
[12] Ibid., 16 July 1887.
[13] *Lincolnshire Chronicle,* 27 June 1862; *Isle of Wight Observer,* 16 November 1912.

LAST YEARS

Through the Babbington Colliery Company, he derived a considerable income from the Nottinghamshire coalfields. He was able to install himself in Sherwood Lodge, an imposing mansion near Arnold, and acquire 3,000 acres of estates across the county. He became a substantial benefactor to the general hospital in Nottingham. On four occasions between 1869 and 1895 Seely was returned for Nottingham as a Liberal and then as a Liberal Unionist. He did not, as he had hoped he might, represent Lincoln after his father's death, but his son, another Charles did, as a Liberal Unionist between 1895 and 1906. When he died in 1915 Sir Charles Seely – he had been created a baronet 19 years beforehand – was one of the richest men in England.[14]

Charles Seely died after a brief illness on 21 October 1887. The celebrated London doctor Sir Andrew Clark had been summoned, but did not arrive in time. On 25 October, 'a bright, calm autumn day', he was interred alongside his wife in the churchyard of St. Mary's, Brooke.[15] In his will he had made provision for his two surviving daughters, each of whom received on trust £50,000 for life, and his widowed son-in-law, who secured £20,000 on trust. On their deaths these life interests, together with an additional legacy of £30,000, were to be divided between the children of his three daughters. The residue of this personal estate was left to his son – who, outside these arrangements, also secured Brooke House and Furzedown House.[16]

What sort of man was Charles Seely? Physically he was a small, thin man, who walked with noticeably long strides. He was missing – presumably after an accident in his youth – a number of fingers on his right hand. This made writing difficult for him, and in the early years of his marriage, he often relied on Mary. Later he employed a private secretary; for many years this was Frank Fellows, who must have known almost as much about Seely as Seely himself did. Seely lived a highly regulated life. 'His walks, riding exercises, business and diet were all attended to with precision', his obituarist recorded, 'and nothing could induce him to swerve from

---

[14] *Nottingham Evening Post,* 16 April 1915.
[15] *Isle of Wight County Press,* 29 October 1887.
[16] *Lincolnshire Chronicle,* 15 November 1887 for a report that, in memory of his father, Seely's son waived for six months the rents he was due from tenants in the Isle of Wight.

executing that which he determined to carry out.'[17] In business Seely was clearly a hard man to deal with. He was equally tenacious in his ambition to enter the House of Commons and, once there, to hold the Board of Admiralty to account. The radical journalist George Jacob Holyoake described Seely as 'a generous, kind-hearted man but without strength of intellectual conviction.'[18] In his later years Seely did indeed turn his back on Liberalism, but once he had been a fiery radical, loathed by the Lincoln Tories. 'At one time he could scarcely walk the streets simply because he fought their battles', a working man recalled. 'It was dangerous to be a Seelyite ...'[19]

---

[17] Ibid., 28 October 1887.
[18] G.J. Holyoake, *Sixty Years of an Agitator's Life*, p. 124.
[19] Ibid., 1 January 1869.

Illustrations

1. Charles Seely. Reproduced by permission of Brook Village History.

2. Charles Seely, with the caption 'Pigs', by Sir Leslie Ward. *Vanity Fair*, 21 December 1878. Copyright the National Portrait Gallery, London.

3. John Hinde Palmer, with the caption 'Lincoln', by Sir Leslie Ward. *Vanity Fair*, 28 July 1883. Palmer contested Lincoln on three occasions before being returned, without a contest and without being aware of his nomination, in November 1868.

4. Thomas Cooper. Seely's champion in the *Stamford Mercury* in the 1830s, he later watched his friend's 'patriotic course in Parliament, and out of it, with intense gratification'.

5. The Stonebow, Lincoln. It was here, whilst reporting on a meeting of the town council of which Seely was a member, that Cooper conceived the idea of writing his epic poem the *Purgatory of Suicides*.

The Horse Fair, Lincoln — Valentines Series

6. The famous Lincoln horse fair. This was a large-scale event, held over a week in April of each year, in which many hundreds of horses were sold.

7. Prince's Gate, London, where Seely lived amongst the London elite.

8. Brooke House, Isle of Wight.

9. The staff employed at Brooke House. Reproduced by permission of Brook Village History.

10. Garibaldi's visit to Brooke House, as depicted by the *Illustrated London News,* 16 April 1864.

Index

Agricultural Holdings Act 1875	33
Ashley, Evelyn	43
'Blunderbuss'	15
Board of Admiralty	27-8, 31
Brooke House	26, 37-41, 54-6
Chaplin, Edward	32
Childers, Hugh	27-8, 31
Clayton & Shuttleworth	17, 19, 21-22, 25, 32, 37
Cooper, Thomas	3, 18, 42, 50-1
Coupland, John	2-3, 17, 22
Ellison, Richard	5-8
Fellows, Frank	45
Furzedown House	37-8, 42
Heighington Hall	35-7
Heneage, Edward	28
Keyworth, J.K.	17, 19, 22
Keyworth, T.M.	4, 17-22, 35
North, Thomas	24
Norton, John	17, 20
Pakington, Sir John	27, 30
Palmer, John Hinde	26, 32, 49
Radford, Joseph	22-3
Railways	12-13
Ruston, Joseph	34
Sanitation	12-13
Seely, Charles	
birth	1
his collieries	20, 22-4
as a councillor	10-12
disillusionment with Liberalism	42-4

INDEX

education	2
election as a mayor	11
election to town council	9-10
and employees	20, 29
his family	35-6, 41, 43, 44-5
and Garibaldi	40-1, 56
in London	37, 53
marriage	3
and naval expenditure	27-33
parents	1-2
and parliamentary election of 1841	14
and parliamentary election of 1847	14-15
and parliamentary election of 1852	15
and parliamentary election of 1857	15-16
and parliamentary election of 1861	26
and parliamentary election of 1865	28
and parliamentary election of 1874	32
and parliamentary election of 1880	33
and parliamentary reform	28, 32
personal characteristics	45-6
philanthropy	3, 33, 36, 39, 40, 44
and pig iron	24-5, 29-30
and Queen Victoria	12, 44
his servants	35-7
his steam mill	4-5, 17-21, 24
and temperance	32-3
and trade unions	23-4
Seely, Charles (son)	1, 44-5
Seely, Charles (grandson)	1, 45
Seely, Mary	36, 41-2, 44-5
Tennyson, Alfred Lord	41
Tweed, J.W.	26

About the Authors

Mark Acton and Stephen Roberts have previously collaborated on *The Parliamentary Career of Charles de Laet Waldo Sibthorp 1826-1855: Ultra-Tory Opposition to Reform in Nineteenth Century Britain* (New York, 2010) and a number of short biographies for the History of Parliament 1832-1868 project. Mark Acton is a member of the Society for Lincolnshire History and Archaeology and Stephen Roberts is affiliated to the Australian National University.

The Birmingham Biographies Series by Stephen Roberts

The Birmingham Biographies Series

Dr J.A. Langford 1823-1903: A Self-Taught Working Man and the Sale of American Degrees in Victorian Britain. £4.99

Sir Benjamin Stone 1838-1914: Photographer, Traveller and Politician. £7.99

Mocking Men of Power: Comic Art in Birmingham 1861-1914. (with Roger Ward). £8.99

Sir Richard Tangye 1833-1906: A Cornish Entrepreneur in Victorian Birmingham. £4.99

Joseph Chamberlain's Highbury: A Very Public Private House. £3.99

Now Mr Editor!: Letters to the Newspapers of Nineteenth Century Birmingham. £6.99

Joseph Gillott: And Four Other Birmingham Manufacturers 1784-1892. £6.99

Birmingham 1889: One year in a Victorian City. £4.99

Recollections of Victorian Birmingham. £4.99

James Whateley and the Survival of Chartism. £4.99

These books can be ordered from Amazon.

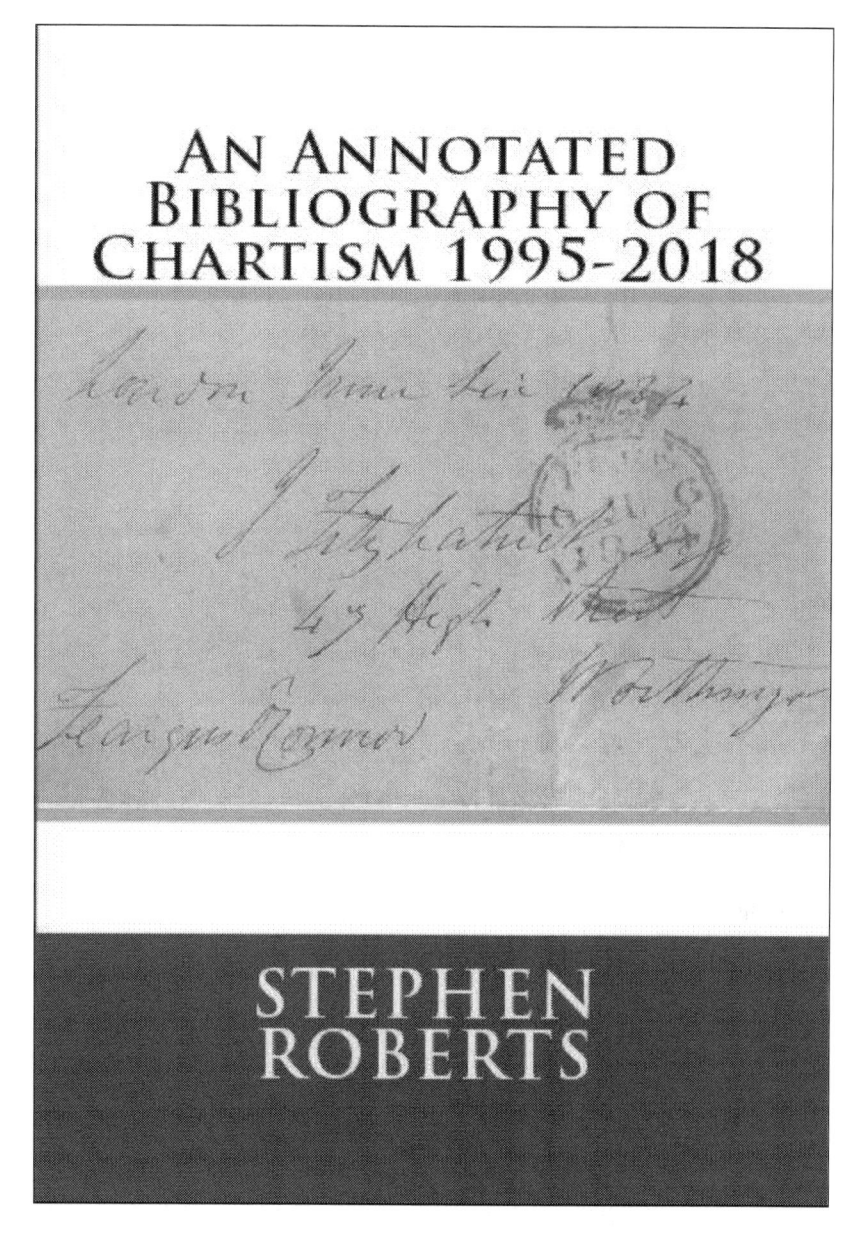

An Annotated Bibliography of Chartism 1995-2018

Stephen Roberts

Available from Amazon, priced £5.02.

Printed in Great Britain
by Amazon